THE JOURNEY ON THE

EDGE OF

MIDNIGHT

by Miss Genny

ISBN: 9781726711029

Any references to historical events, real people, or real places are used fictitiously. Names, characters, and places are products of the author's imagination.

Front cover image by K&T Graphics

www.kandtgraphicdesigns.com

First printing edition 2018

Dedication

I would like to dedicate this book to those families who are going through with their family members in hospice. I also dedicate this book to all of the doctors, nurses, certified nursing assistants, home health aides, facilities, and hospitals who give their all to hospice patients.

There is life after death and I will continue to help those patients who need hospice assistance to make their journey home.

Acknowledgements

First, I want to thank our Lord and Savior Jesus Christ. Without Him pushing and encouraging me through others, letting me know that I could write this book, it would never have happened. It was not until He let me know, "I told you years ago to write; you are walking in disobedience," did I say, "Yes, Lord."

I want to thank Pastor William W. Simmons Sr for speaking to me ten years ago, after I had given a message to our congregation, letting me know that I needed to write a short book.

To my friend Stephanie who really encouraged me and supported me during the times when fear and doubt would grip me, and I'd say, "I just can't do this, I'm not a writer." She'd say, "Just tell your story."

Keith inspired me after reading one of his books titled *Meditation Times with Elma.* Oh, what a love story!

Karen, CEO of Critique Editing Services, who held my hand, encouraged and waited patiently on me and talked me through my fears and doubting moments. Thank you, Karen.

I must thank the dear, exciting speaker who introduced me to Karen, Miss Anteia Greer.

Foreword

Prepare for an experience.

Genevieve takes us into a frontier that most people don't voluntarily enter. It's "the edge of Midnight," that borderland between life and death that we'll all enter for ourselves at some point, or sooner than that maybe—as often happens—have occasion to be drawn there through the near-death time of a loved one.

But Genevieve and that rare breed of hospice workers enter "The Edge" by choice—or even better—by calling. Genny's particular calling of God is that of "chaplain." Even at that, her experiences may tend to be different; for Genny has a sense of God's Spirit, present and directing in this Borderland, that all won't necessarily have.

So, in this little book, she takes you with her to the bedsides of Walter, and Alice, and John and others, to help them make "that crossing" between life and eternity. She has the help of what is a team of RNs and co-workers, who alert each other and pray with each other for their varied patients.

She uniquely engages with her patients and their families, some who are very reluctant to have her around—some, since she's African American. Color isn't always the difficulty. Other times, it's just the fear of dying itself and other complicating circumstances. Whatever, you'll find her experiences to be sometimes funny, often sobering, and even heartwarming.

And you're in for a few surprising ones if you choose to enter this "Journey on the Edge of Midnight" along with Chaplain Genevieve McGuire.

O. Keith Hueftle,
Christian conference director,
retired pastor and former client
of Chaplain Genevieve McGuire

Table of Contents

Introduction

Hospice is a special concept of care designed to provide comfort and support to patients and their families when a life-limiting illness no longer responds to cure-oriented treatments. This type of care neither prolongs life nor hastens death. While it addresses all symptoms of a disease, hospice places a special emphasis on controlling a patient's pain and discomfort. Hospice aids with the emotional, social and spiritual impact of diseases on the patient and that of the patient's family and friends.

In addition, hospice offers a variety of bereavement and counseling services to families before and after a patient's death. It is not restricted to an actual specific facility but is also offered in the patient's home.

Chapter 1:
He Will Beautify the Meek

"For the LORD taketh pleasure in his people: he will beautify the meek with salvation." Psalm 149:4

As a chaplain I have seen the hand of God move upon people in what I refer to as the 11:45 hour. God has blessed me to experience some very awesome things while performing my duties as a hospice chaplain. Let me share with you such an experience. My supervisor requested that I go see a patient who was in a long-term care facility. When I went to visit this patient, I found a diminutive lady who was in her 80s, with a heavily wrinkled face that was accentuated by her striking white hair.

I introduced myself to this frail, soft-spoken lady. She was very weak and spoke only above a whisper. I asked, "Do you love Jesus?" Her answer was "Yes." I then asked,

"Do you have the Lord in your heart?"

She hesitated but finally said, "Yes." Her hesitation, however, made me feel uneasy. I said, "Sweetheart, would you like to know for sure that you will have eternal life with Him when you die?" Again, she answered, "Yes." She confessed her sins and asked God to forgive her and be Lord over her life. We ended our visit with prayer.

A week later my supervisor informed me that this dear lady was dying, and family members could not be there for her. I rushed to the facility and went directly to the room that I had visited a week earlier. I learned that she had been moved to another room and was given the room number by a nurse. As I walked into the room, I noticed that it was shared by two elderly women. I stopped at the first bed because the occupant looked like my patient from the previous visit. I spoke to her and when she began to talk with me, I thought to myself, *If she is actively dying (with death being imminent), how can she hold a conversation this well?*

I looked at the other lady in the next bed and recognized the oxygen equipment as being the type of equipment that we use, but the lady looked about 20 years younger. She had no wrinkles—and I mean no wrinkles at all.

I went back to the nurse to see if I had gone to the right room.

The nurse answered, "Yes, she is by the window." I went back to the room, where I made an amazing discovery. The lady with the smooth skin was indeed my patient! She was actively dying, but God had already stepped in.

He had beautifully transformed her! I started to pray quietly for her to help her cross over. There appeared to be some sort of battle going on as I prayed.

I continued to pray and noticed the lady in the other bed was making a lot of noise and talking to herself. Suddenly I noticed that the room felt totally different; a peaceful, calm presence was there: The room became brighter and the roommate had become quiet.

I read Psalm 23.

"The Lord is my Shepherd; I shall not want.

He makes me to lie down in green pastures;

He leads me beside the still waters.

He restores my soul;

He leads me in the paths of righteousness

for His name's sake.

Yea, though I walk through the valley

of the shadow of death,

I will fear no evil: for you are with me:

Your rod and Your staff, they comfort me.

You prepare a table before me

in the presence of my enemies;

You anoint my head with oil;

My cup runs over,

Surely goodness and mercy shall follow me

All the days of my life:

And I will dwell in the house of the Lord Forever."

I then started singing "Swing Low, Sweet Chariot."

By that time, the hospice registered nurse had arrived. She pulled the covers back and asked me, "Have you ever seen anything like this?" I answered, "No, this is my first experience." The patient had started to turn purple on the feet and legs, and purple had begun to appear in her fingertips, which is called mottling. The hospice nurse told me that the patient would be gone in about half an hour. I immediately took the patient's hand and whispered in her ear. "It's okay, you can go and be with Jesus," I said. "Everything is okay." The patient was experiencing shortness of breath.

I looked away for a few minutes, and when I looked back, I adjusted my glasses because I couldn't believe . . . The peace. The glow, the lack of wrinkles, and darkness of hair that I was observing.

The patient then took her last breath.

Chapter 2:
Secrets in the Attic

"If we confess our sins, he is faithful and just to forgive us our sins, and to cleanse us from all unrighteousness." 1 John 1:9

We all have made mistakes and made wrong choices not knowing the consequences could torment us a lifetime.

Victoria was in her late 80s. I made repeated visits to have prayer, scripture reading and companionship with her. One day Victoria said, "I can trust you with my secret." She looked at me and I said, "What is it, baby girl?" She said, "I don't believe Jesus will forgive me." I said, "But we have prayed and asked him." She said, "I did the unforgiveable." I said, "Baby, no matter what it is, He has forgiven you because you asked Him to."

She said, "Well when I was in my early 20s, I had an abortion." I said, "The bible tells us that if we confess our sins, He is a just God and will forgive us and you have done that even before today. We have prayed for all of your sins to be forgiven." She took a deep breath and said, "But I had *two* abortions." I said again, "He has forgiven you." Then she stared out into space as if to relive the past and slowly said, "He was a married man." I took her hand and said, "And you are *still* forgiven." She said, "I can't believe it unless I see it in black and white." I took a white napkin and wrote, "You are forgiven," with a black pen and told her to keep it until she could believe.

I made numerous trips to see her and each time I'd ask if she still had it, and she would pull it out and say, "I just don't believe He will forgive me." I was very concerned, so I prayed and asked God to truly help her. She had been tormented by this long enough with the shame and guilt. I needed Him to give her peace, joy and happiness during this season of her life. She had carried pain, shame, and hurt for over sixty-some years and it was past time for the tormenting devil to back off. I seriously interceded in prayer.

I made my usual visit one day and I could tell immediately that she was different. I said, "Do you still have your napkin?" She said, "No." I said, "Do you believe?" She said, "Yes." She added that she had a peace she didn't have before and had no idea where the napkin was. I said, "You don't need it any longer. Now you believe." Victoria got better and graduated from hospice. One day several years later, I received a call that she had passed, and she had left instructions for me to have words at her service. I attended the service and it was the first and only open-casket graveside service I had ever experienced. There she lay in the most beautiful royal blue dress with nothing but peace, sweet peace on her face. No more secrets in the attic.

To God be the Glory!

I faced a different set of challenges with each patient and each case.

Chapter 3:
I'm Going to Marry Jesus

"Let us be glad and rejoice and give Him glory, for the marriage

of the Lamb has come, and His wife has made herself ready."

Revelation 19:7

I must tell you about Alice. Oh what a dear, dear sweet lady. I remember walking into her home, where she lived with her daughter and her family and standing beside her bed. As I spoke with her about death and dying, she looked at me and said, "And you are going to help me?" I smiled, and she began to tell me and the nurse her story and her fears and concerns.

Something had happened to Alice that was so devastating to her, she felt that when she got to heaven her husband was not going to want her. As she confided her concerns to us, we assured her everything would be all right. And then the very last thing that Alice and I talked about was that *she was going to be married to Jesus.*

After her transition, Alice's family asked me to perform the service, even though she had a pastor. He wasn't able to perform the services that day, but he assured the family he would be there.

The day of the services Alice's pastor and I met in the vestibule of the church. As we introduced ourselves, he stated, "I will walk down the aisle with you and escort you to the pulpit." When the music started, he grabbed my arm and we proceeded to walk. It was like I was being escorted in a wedding, and I could hear Alice saying, "I'm going to go and be married to Jesus."

I had never experienced anything like it. As we walked down the aisle and stopped at the casket before going up to the podium, I looked at Alice. She was in the most beautiful red dress. And there was a radiant glow all around her. There was no doubt in my mind that Alice's desire had been fulfilled.

During the sermon, the family received a phone call that Alice's great grandchild Chance had been born. What a glorious day for the family.

To God be the glory for the things He has done.

Chapter 4:
A Heart Re-Created New

"Create in me a clean heart, O God, and renew a steadfast spirit

within me." Psalm 51:10

Oh, I must tell you about Walter.

I went to Walter's house to make an assessment. Walter and his lovely wife and I sat at the kitchen table. Walter answered my questions for the assessment and then began to tell me he didn't need me. He had his pastor and he was all right spiritually. I told him politely that was just fine, and if he needed me, I would be there for him and his family.

Well, whenever the nurse would make a visit to see Walter, she would come back and say, "Genny, Walter needs you." And I would say, "Walter says he is okay and doesn't need me, and I will not be pushy. Everyone is entitled to make their own choice."

Well, the day came that the nurse said, "I have convinced Walter to see you again."

I went to see Walter, and I sat at the kitchen table and began to tell Walter about things that happened to him as a child. I told him he needed emotional healing and to let the past go before he passed away. Walter began weeping. He said nobody knew those things about him but his wife. I said, "God knows and has spoken this to me—your wife didn't tell me."

From then on, I was in Walter's home every Friday for a month, praying for him. He called all his children and siblings; he wanted everyone in the family to be healed of the past.

One of the reasons Walter didn't want me to help him initially was because he had prejudice in his heart. One Friday he admitted this to me. I looked at him and just smiled, knowing that all was well.

He was broken in his heart. Psalm 51:17 states, "The sacrifice that God wants is a humble spirit. God, you will not turn away someone who comes with a humble heart and is willing to obey you."

Walter was freeing himself up to live with Jesus. So many people just need their souls healed.

What Are You Doing In Your D-A-S-H?

If you are reading this book, you are in your *D-A-S-H,* and if you have ever gone to a cemetery and looked at some of the headstones, you will see a name printed there with the date of birth; then there is a D-A-S-H, just waiting for you to complete your journey of life. You are living in your D-A-S-H.

I want to encourage all of you to get your past and your present together so that the future is guaranteed.

I had prayed and met different members of his family by phone or in person, as I spent time with him every Friday for a month. The last Friday I was in the house, I told the son Chris, "Okay, it's *your* time." I allowed God to use me to speak into his life and told him to pick up the mantle and do what his dad was supposed to do, and that was to minister to people and preach the gospel. I prayed for Chris and he repented and did just that, traveling overseas and in the Tri-State area, building God's Kingdom.

Before Walter passed, I would talk to him about the six o'clock hour in the evening. I told him that was the time I would look in the sky for Jesus.

If I needed to talk with Jesus or was distraught after a long day, I would look in the heavens and say, "I need you. I need to see you. I need to know you are present with me." I would look into the heavens, and the clouds would start moving, and there would be the beautiful colors of the rainbow. It was Him letting me know, "I'm here."

When the weather was good and the entrance to the river was open, I would drive down to the river, park my car, run up the hill and sit on the bench and look for Him saying, "I need you." And sure enough, the clouds would start turning and swirling into those beautiful rainbow colors. I would just sit there and talk with Him in my mind, letting Him know just how I felt, and letting go of all the grief and cares that I was carrying.

You see there was no way I could see the things that I saw in the spirit realm, and minister to the patients, sometimes getting emotionally involved with them, and not cry out to Him. I recognize I need His help and His help alone.

I had talked with all Walter's family members. He and I sat side by side in his family room, arms locked, smiling at each other because his heart was right. There were no longer any color barriers—only that *agape* love toward each other.

One evening I got a call; Walter was transitioning fast. I was with another patient and was trying to get to him as fast as I could, but when I arrived at Walter's home, he was gone. His lovely wife Sue looked at me and said, "Genny, he remembered what you said. It was 6 p.m. when he took his last breath."

That family is still in my life. Chris is now married and invited me to his wedding and emailed me from the delivery room. He and his wife have had their first baby. One daughter will be getting married soon, and I've had a chance to meet the fiancé and pray showers of blessing over him. Walter's lovely wife is busy in ministry and we run into each other from time to time. He touched me, and He made me whole.

Chapter 5:
Supernatural Change

"If a man dies, shall he live again? All the days of my hard

service I will wait, Till my change comes." Job 14:14

Let's talk about John.

I went to meet John at his home and made the usual

required company assessment. I informed John that we had a

male chaplain and that if he would feel more comfortable with

him, I would understand. John said, "No, you will be okay."

I made small talk with John and then began to ask him

how he was spiritually. He stated he was okay: He watched TV

church and said when they would pray, he would pray with them.

Well, about two weeks later I received a phone call from

John stating that he needed to see me. I asked him what the

problem was. He stated, "I need to be sure I'm going to heaven."

I said, "Well, I will be there." I arrived at John's house, we talked, and he stated he just felt like he needed to be sure he was going to heaven.

Now, John was in a hospital bed, and he had on a pair of blue flannel checkered pajamas. His hair was black mixed with gray. I stood by John's bed to pray with him.

I normally don't close my eyes when praying for a patient, but this time I did. I opened my mouth, and words poured out of me that I had no intention of saying, and they just kept flowing. It was the most beautiful prayer for someone to receive salvation I had ever prayed. (I kept thinking, "I need to record this.")

I opened my eyes and was shocked: There lay John—in a long white robe with lines about an inch wide going down it. His hair was completely white, and he was illuminated. My eyes were wide. I pulled my glasses up and down. And I heard God say very plainly, "Tell him everything is all right." I was so amazed, I whispered, and I said, "God said everything is alright." I blinked my eyes again and things were back to normal.

John said he believed and knew he was okay, and all I knew was if he didn't, I sure did. I had never—and I mean never—experienced anything in the spirit like that in my life. I shall never forget.

His Grace and Mercy

Chapter 6:
Put on the New Man

"And that you put on the new man which was created according to God, in true righteousness and holiness." Ephesians 4:24

As you know, not everyone wants Jesus in their lives. And we've had situations where the RN would say, "Genny, his heart isn't ready, and I can't get him to see you."

Well, whenever we came across situations like this, each morning before we started to work, the team had to have a conference call, and we would all pray that God would touch that particular patient's heart so that they would receive salvation before they died. Our goal was to never let anyone die without Jesus if we could prevent it. We are determined that everyone will go to heaven.

The patient was beginning to get close. The RN was getting desperate. She came into the office and said, "Genny, you have got to pray that God touches his heart. He is getting close and he still refuses to see you."

I prayed; the team prayed.

Yep, the RN texted me and said, "He has consented for you to come." It was 4 P.M. I said, "Do you want me to wait until tomorrow?" She said, "No, Genny. I don't know if he will make it until tomorrow."

Well I jumped into my car, traveled about 20 miles, and walked into the dark house. He was lying in the bed. Boy was death ever present! I told him who I was and told him that Jesus loved him. I said I needed him to pray with me and mean it in his heart and ask Jesus to forgive him of all his sins—and he did. After he prayed, I prayed for him that he would have a peaceful sleep because he hadn't been resting and was very tormented at night.

That was Thursday. I was told the next day he had a good night. Well, that weekend he passed. I wanted to go to the visitation because God has gifted me to see if everything was okay in their hearts. I walked into the visitation, spoke with the family, walked up to the casket and—truly, again—I couldn't believe my eyes. That man looked twenty-some years younger, and the family saw it too. One family member said, "When I get ready to die, I want you to come pray for me because we know he accepted Jesus." The RN was so glad. She said, "Genny, he looked so nice."

All I can say is God wants everyone, so He keeps working with you and giving you a chance to say *yes* to Him.

Chapter 7:
Don't Let It Be Said Too Late

"Afterward the other virgins came also, saying. Lord, Lord, open to us! But he answered and said, Assuredly, I say to you, I do not know you. Watch therefore, for you know neither the day nor the hour in which the Son of Man is coming." Matthew 25:11-13

I must tell you, not everyone has a happy ending.

I remember getting called to go to the hospital because a young man was dying. I went to see him and prayed for him. He asked Jesus to forgive him, and Jesus touched him. He got out of the hospital, went to the nursing facility for rehab, got out of there, got his own apartment and was doing good. He started living his old lifestyle, not acknowledging Jesus anymore.

This went on for a while, I tried to talk to him. He would say he was okay with God. One day I got a call that he was in the hospital. I took a couple other people with me. Death had him; he was struggling to breathe. It was what I call "ugly death." His face was distorted, and the atmosphere was not good. I prayed, but I just couldn't reach him. He died, and it wasn't a peaceful sight or death.

He had taken life and God for granted, and there was nothing I could do. We are to be prepared, faithful and responsible in our walk with the Lord. Jesus teaches the necessity of preparedness for His return. He compares his coming to a joyful wedding procession in which the unprepared cannot participate. We don't know when Jesus is coming; we must be like the wise virgins and stay prepared and not like the foolish who were "TOO LATE!"

Chapter 8:
What's in Your Heart?

"Today, if you will hear His voice, Do not harden your

hearts as in the rebellion."

On another occasion, I had a patient, and his wife and I were constantly asking him to ask Jesus to forgive him. He would just ignore us.

Well, he passed. I went to the visitation, and when I looked in the casket, all I could see was a spirit of pride lying there. And we know that pride will not enter into God's sight.

We came in without earthly possessions and pure in heart, and that is the way God will accept us—with nothing and pure in heart.

You see, this journey is all about the heart. He tells us plainly in the Bible how to live our daily lives: without anger, bitterness, unforgiveness, prejudice, malice, hatred, adultery, idolatry, fornication, murder and—just to sum it up—sin. Yes, we all have fallen short, but it's when you continue to blatantly sin and think you're going to heaven anyhow is when your heart isn't right and connected to God.

Yes, He is a merciful God, but He is also just and means what He says when He says to obey his word.

We all have gotten hurt in life. And life has been harder on some than others, and we have allowed things to get into our hearts that will actually keep us from getting into the door of heaven. But during the journey, allow Him to do a washing and cleansing to make us fit for His world.

Chapter 9:
The Color Barrier

"But you be watchful in all things, endure afflictions, do the work of an evangelist, fulfill your ministry." 2 Timothy 4:5

There was a time when I felt persecuted because of being female and African American.

I made a visit to a patient's home. His wife was very nice, but he wasn't very friendly. I was trying to get a spiritual assessment from him, and he really didn't want to look at me or talk with me. His wife was trying to make up for his behavior. Finally the patient stated he needed to go to the restroom, so that I would leave.

When our RN made her next visit to see the patient, he told her not to let me come back because I had been "in the sun too long."

A few months went by, and I received a call from one of our nurses, asking me to make a visit to see this patient again. I informed the RN that I had gone to see this patient, and he stated he didn't want to see me "because I had been in the sun too long." Her reply was, "Genny, his wife is asking for you, and he is now in a facility." I did not want to go, but I knew I had a job to do.

When I arrived at the facility, there were a lot of people standing outside, near the door. I figured that was his family, and I couldn't stop thinking of those words, "She has been in the sun too long." So I hurried into the facility to the patient's room.

His wife, daughter and other family members were standing around his bedside. I spoke and inquired about the patient and was saying in my head, "God, what am I here for? What do you want me to do with a man dying who doesn't even want me around?"

I spoke with the spouse, had prayer and asked the family if they wanted to join in with the prayer. I felt horrible; I asked the wife, "Have you called your pastor?" She said, "Yes, he was just here."

Well, that did it.

I began talking to God in my head, *What am I here for? Their pastor has been here. They don't need me.* And I sure was feeling very uncomfortable.

On the other side of the curtain was another one of my patients. I needed to escape the environment I was in, so I stepped over to the other side of the curtain and began to sing to the other patient because he loved hearing me sing. And I felt I needed to do something to get my emotions under control and clear all the negative vibes I was feeling.

I sang to the other patient until I was at peace and calm.

When I went back to the other side of the curtain, the wife said, "That was beautiful. Will you sing to my husband?" I didn't want to, but I did, and I gave her encouraging words then left. The patient never really acknowledged me being there.

When I got in the car, I asked God, "Okay, what was that all about? I felt humiliated, and his pastor had been there, and I didn't even need to be there." God was quiet and didn't join in my conversation at all.

Well the next day, I went to see a patient in the same small town who was pleasant to be with, and we both enjoyed our visits. I left happy and felt it was a "job well done." As I drove down the highway, God spoke to me and said: "Stop at the facility and see the patient you visited last night." I immediately said, "No, God! No!" He spoke back and said, "Are you only going to love those that love you?" Wow! What a blow. I felt small and ashamed.

I stopped at the facility. I wasn't glad about it and didn't know what I was doing with this patient again.

This time the only person in the room was the daughter. She said, "Would you like to sit over here where I'm sitting to be close to him?" I said, "No, I'm fine standing." Before I knew it, I had leaned over the patient and told him that God loved him and that I loved him and that love and forgiveness in our hearts was what we needed to get into heaven. He moved his arm up toward me and I backed away because I didn't know if he was going to hit me.

His daughter said, "He wants to hug you." Well, I was shocked and very unsure of that, so I prayed and sang a song and left.

When I got to the office, I was told by one of the home health aides that the patient had asked God into his heart earlier that morning before I got there. Well, I felt small again. God said, "See! Had you looked past your emotions the night before and reached out to the family in love, you have no idea what would have happened to their hearts."

Yes, it was a learning experience that I will never forget. It's not about me. It's what God can do through me and with me, so that someone can be set free.

Chapter 10:
A Renewed Mind

"And do not be conformed to this world, but be transformed by the renewing of your mind, that you may prove what is that good and acceptable and perfect will of God." Roman 12:2

I must tell you about another patient that had a problem with color, but we knew he needed Jesus. He started to decline, and he had a mild case of dementia. I had made a visit to assess him and was told by the nurse afterwards that he wasn't "fond of my race."

As time went by he started to decline, and the RN wanted him to have a visit before he really started declining mentally. I was informed he had good days and bad days with the dementia. Since we work as a team, the RN stated she felt it would be okay for me to visit. She added that she felt he just needed to talk about some things that needed to be addressed before he left this world.

I started praying before I made the visit that God would touch his heart and that he would accept me and be kind. I also asked God to open the windows of his mind to understand.

You see, there is nothing too hard or impossible with God. With my patients who have dementia, even before I get to them, I pray and ask God to deal with their minds, so that they will be receptive to what I have to say to them. I also pray the patient will have clarity and understanding to ask Him to forgive them, and most of the time He will honor the request.

When I arrived, there was clarity of mind. He understood and could remember. I had been told by the nurse of our team that he was dealing with unforgiveness regarding his ex-wife. I discussed this with him, and he admitted there was a problem. I asked him if we could pray about his struggles and he said, "Yes." I discussed the Lord's Prayer and what it says and means about forgiveness because he had informed me that he was Catholic and wanted to pray The Lord's Prayer. Before praying, I began to break the prayer down and discuss love and forgiveness—because I knew he also had a problem with prejudice. I explained about God's unconditional love and forgiveness.

I continued to pray with him during each visit. Changes began to take place in his heart.

The last visit I made, he informed me that he had forgiven his ex-wife and the feelings he had toward me were gone and thanked me for the time I had spent with him. Yes, he was heaven-ready. He knew it, and I knew it.

Chapter 11:
A Change Has Come Into My Life

"In my distress I cried to the Lord, And He heard me."

Psalm 120:1

Let's talk about Tommy, who came to our services wheel chair bound and handicap with speech.

My heart went out to him. He was at life's end with other health complications and could hardly speak to let his needs be understood clearly. I made a visit with him and had a very hard time understanding what he was saying, but we eventually made it through and completed the assessment.

I left concerned and just wanted God to give him another chance at life with the care that he was now getting at this facility. He was given six months and was declining. I told my supervisor, "I really want him to live and start to have clear speech and another chance at life." She stated, "Genny, it doesn't look good for him." I said, "well, I just believe."

I continued to pray. I made another visit and I started asking him to take his time to pronounce words and to repeat them after me. He tried hard and made it to the end. I asked him, "Do you love Jesus and want Him in your heart?" He said, "Yes." I had him repeat the sinner's prayer the best he could. God knew his heart.

I got word the facility nurse came in one night and he was on his knees on the floor. They thought he had fallen on the floor because he had to have assistance to get up. When they asked if that was what happened, he said, "No, Praying." I continued to visit and one of our RN made visual aide cards so that he could point at pictures so we all could communicate better with him, but I continue to help him say his words slowly.

I was informed that Tommy wanted to be baptized. There was a chaplain at the facility that did Sunday morning services with the residents and I went to him and ask if he could make this happen and he did. Tommy was over joyed the residents were there it was such a joyful time.

Tommy came off hospice services. No, he's not completely well physically, but he's happy, eats well and has his second chance with his soul connected with Jesus.

Chapter 12:
Joan and Darby

"Have you not read that He who made them at the beginning made them male and female and said 'For this reason a man shall leave his father and mother and be joined to his wife, and the two shall become one flesh?' Therefore what God has joined together, let no man separate." Matthew 19:4-6

Joan was one of my intriguing patients and Darby was the most amazing in-love man I have every experienced in Hospice. Joan had dementia and I had no idea the journey I was about to take with this most in-love fascinating couple.

First of all Darby was not going to let Joan leave him without a fight. When I did Joan's assessment, I spoke with Darby and let him know that Joan was now on Hospice and he needed to prepare to let her go. Well, at that time he looked at me and said, "I understand." Well, he might have understood, but he was in love like I've never seen a man in love before and in his mind, *she will live!* He began to do whatever it was going to take.

Darby realized he needed care as well, and he wanted to be close to the bride of his youth. He moved into the assisted-living section of the same facility. He was determined to be the mouthpiece, eyes, ears and whatever else Joan needed on this journey.

He was crushed at heart when his beloved was sent out for treatment to another city and another facility and came back home worse than she was when she left. Well, he was ready for action. He started a daily routine with her and made sure to the best of his ability to make whatever time she had left the best. He would hold her in his arms, sing, pray and read scripture to her. They talked about the past and the future.

The most adorable thing was when I came to visit one day, and he said he had told Joan, "We've never been old before, and all of this is new to us. We've just got to learn to trust God in this thing, too."

I would visit once a month. My heart was broken as I watched this man keeping his wife alive with love. One day I said, "Darby, you must write all that you are doing in this relationship. The Bible says, 'Until death do you part,' and this type of love and care that you are giving Joan, I have never experienced before. You must share how you are keeping her alive when she should have been gone so many times."

Darby would listen to me, but didn't comply, so one day I became very demanding. "Darby, you must tell the other husbands and wives that are on the same journey as you—and those that have yet to face this journey—how to be patient and understanding with their loved one and all the details of caring and loving."

One day I made a visit, and Darby told me he had written their obituaries. Darby wanted to leave when Joan left, and he was prepared. I spoke to Darby and I informed him, "Darby, your time isn't up. There are too many men out in this world that need the wisdom and knowledge that God has given you to love until death do you part."

Joan was in a facility that gave her care, but Darby worked so hard taking care of Joan, he became sick, and his children took them to their home in Indianapolis to get some rest. He was physically, mentally and emotionally exhausted.

Joan began to want to go home to Jesus, and she was doing her best to tell Darby. She was beginning to sleep a lot and eat less. He finally began to accept that she would depart without him. Thanksgiving came, and the family came to visit late in the day. Joan showed very little response. The family stayed over the weekend. Joan's breathing pattern had begun to change. The family didn't know if they should stay or leave. (You see, Joan had done this before, and then she would improve.) It was hard, but the family said their goodbyes.

Darby stayed. He had his supper tray beside hers, sang songs and read scripture to her. Oh, what dedication!

The hospice nurse urged Darby to go to his apartment; Joan was resting in her room, and he needed his rest. So Darby had his nightly routine of saying their prayers, and then he'd kiss her goodnight. He returned to his room and went to sleep. This faithful, beloved husband was tired.

Darby was awakened by the night nurse who said, "Joan is gone." He said he dressed and made the usual trip down the hall to see her and hug her (still warm), giving her face-hugs and praises to God. He remembered hearing that "The hearing is the last to go," so he talked and sang to her, believing she heard him, and he told her how much he loved her.

I imagine in my mind Darby saying, "I'll always love you," and God saying to Darby, "Well done, thou good and faithful servant! Well Done!"

Chapter 13:
Can You Believe And Trust

"Trust in the Lord with all your heart, and lean not on your own understanding; In all your ways acknowledge Him, And He shall direct your paths." Proverbs 3:5

I remember going to the patient's home. I introduced myself and I felt so much peace about the patient. I said, "Do you believe in healing?" He said the nurse had just left before I came in and had told him he had about three months. I said, "What faith are you?" He told me what he used to be. I said, "You know what? I don't see death on you. We are going to build your faith up and believe God!"

I went back for a second visit, and he told me that his daughter told him that when I made the first visit and was coming into the door, she saw a halo around me. Well, I prayed at each visit and sang songs.

He had to have surgery, and he and his wife were worried. The doctor had said he had a 50/50 chance. We prayed, and God did it again. He came out just fine.

He began to improve, and—you guessed it—he was terminated from hospice. This patient lived seven more years.

Chapter 14:
Hope

"On the third day you shall go up to the house of the Lord. And I will add to your days fifteen years." 2 Kings 20:5

Jane was a cookie maker and she could make the best sugar cookies. Jane lived in a trailer park, but as time went along, she couldn't stay by herself, so she had to move into a facility. Jane had gotten so used to the nurses, CNAs, chaplains and social workers all coming to see her, we became her family and she enjoyed all that attention. She had hope in her life.

There was another chaplain working with me and he would go visit Jane monthly. She was declining fast, hadn't eaten in three days, and he suggested I go see her. I went to the facility and the hospice nurse, chaplain and social worker were all there. I said, "Jane, do you see the angels?" She said, "No," in a very, very weak voice. I said, "Do you want to go be with Jesus?" She was very still. All of a sudden, she spoke up with a loud voice and said, "No," and said she wanted to live.

They got her some water and Jane decided to live. Jane loved the attention we gave her. She made up in her mind, *I'm not going to give up this right now.* Jane continued to improve, so much so she no longer qualified for hospice services. The chaplain said, "Genny, I believe God is going to extend her life at least five more years." Since Jane wasn't on our services any longer and our other patient demands were so critical, we didn't see her often unless one of our critical patients was in the facility that Jane was in.

I would stop to see Jane sometimes, and I was told she wasn't the happy person she used to be. She stayed in her room a lot, she wouldn't eat with the other residents or socialize with them, and some in the facility stated she was being mean to them. However when we would visit, she was her old self. I often wondered about that night when she made the choice; did she make the right choice? Well, Jane lived five years to the day of the last incident.

Chapter 15:
The Chicken Dance

"Rejoice in the Lord Always. Again, I will say, rejoice!"

Philippians 3:9

So many times, the patients and their families have you crying and laughing all at the same time.

I was once called out during the wee hours of the morning. One of my patients was dying and the family and patient needed support. I walked into the patient's room, and she was restless. Her two daughters stated they had been praying. Their mother was ready to go.

I sang a medley of songs to her and talked and prayed with her to let her know it was okay: her daughters and family would be okay. I let her know she had nothing here on this Earth to be concerned about. I said, "Baby, it is truly okay."

She began to cross over. Just as she was leaving, her grandson's wife came into the room and draped herself over her and said, "Grandma, Grandma, don't leave me." The patient struggled. She wanted to leave, she wanted to stay. But she forced herself to come back.

The daughters both looked at me and really couldn't believe what had just happened.

The young lady left after she had spent her time with the patient. The daughters explained to me that she and her grandma were very close. They looked at me. They loved their mother, but they realized she no longer had quality of life. They said: "What do we do now?"

"You two go for a walk and pray," I said. "I'm going to talk and pray with your mom."

I prayed and talked with the patient, and she went to sleep. I sat with her until her daughters got back. I asked them if they were okay and both replied, "Yes." I let them know I would leave and come back later that morning. So, they also left the room.

I was walking down the hallway, almost to the exit door, and realized I had left my song book, so I went back. When I walked in, I glanced at the patient and, lo and behold, *she was transitioning out of here again*. I went to the lounge and told the girls, "Come back in here! She is leaving us."

We all were beside the bed. I grabbed the patient's hand and said, "Come on, baby. Look up and see Jesus and grab His hand. You can do this. Keep looking and stay focused. Go ahead. take his hand." She stared up at the ceiling, and her eyes were wide. She blinked and was gone.

Oh, what a glorious moment. But that's not all. The family wanted me to officiate the services. It was a large family that didn't want anything sad. They knew Mom was with Jesus, and it was time to celebrate her life. They stated she loved the Chicken Dance, and at the end of the services they wanted to be in charge.

Well, the day came. I provided services with scripture reading, singing and sermon. At the end I just said, "Family, *you're on.*" The music started, and everyone lined up and the dancing began. Oh, what a joyful celebration they had. Yes, there were tears, but tears of joy and hope for her future.

Now, that's the way to end The Journey.

About the Author

Genevieve, well known to many as "Miss Genny," was born in Evansville, Indiana. She lived the majority of her adult life in Indianapolis, Indiana where she reared a son Roderick and a daughter LaShan.

Genevieve graduated from the C. H. Mason Bible Jurisdictional Institute. She is very active in her church and is the president of the Young Women's Christian Council, where she mentors and teaches young women in the ways of righteous living. She reaches the masses with seminars and biblical counseling, equipping and empowering men and women to face the crises of this generation.

Genevieve is an ordained chaplain who works as a bereavement coordinator in hospice care and also reaches out to men and women in pre- and post-abortion challenges. Genevieve truly loves the Lord and comes from a strong Christian background. *Journey on the Edge of Midnight* is her first literary project.

My story of *The Journey on the Edge of Midnight* is a compilation of some of my God-filled encounters with patients in my position as chaplain in hospice. Hospice has allowed me to truly experience God as I cared for these patients physically, emotionally, and most importantly, spiritually beyond what the natural eye can see, feel and comprehend. I've gone into dimensions in God that I never knew existed and it is my desire to share these encounters with the world.

The road that I've traveled has allowed me to experience God's unconditional love towards mankind, which has been overwhelming at times. It has allowed me to prepare and assist my patients with their transition to the next life, which means I've had to be courageous and bold in the face of spiritual battles. With all of this I wanted to share my story of God and how His strength takes control when we are at our most vulnerable point in life.

Once you've read this book there will be no doubt in your mind as to the reality of God and His desire to connect with His people. Use this book to encourage yourself, a family member, lend it to caregivers, read it to the dying, give it as a gift. *The Journey on the Edge of Midnight* is sure to make you think, "I must be about my Father's business."

Made in the USA
Columbia, SC
17 November 2024

46446046R00038